A Boy
Who Came Home

by

WILLIAM F. ERICSON

Lieutenant, United States Marine Air Corps

New York 1947

CONTENTS

A BOY WHO CAME HOME

Then said He unto them, "Therefore every scribe which is instructed unto the kingdom of heaven is like unto a man that is an householder, which bringeth forth out of his treasure, things new and old." Matthew 13:52

FOREWORD

This is how William Forssell Ericson, who left this world on October 6, 1943, came to write a message of truth and hope for the world in January, 1946.

Bill, as we called him, was born September 14, 1921. A beautiful baby grew into a lovely lad, then a charming handsome man. He was nearly six feet tall, broad-shouldered, well-built, with russet-gold hair which earned him the nickname, "Red." He had large hazel eyes, shaded by long lashes. His mouth and chin were beautifully chiseled. He had a pleasing bass voice and was always singing about the house.

While in high school he belonged to the Richmond Men's Glee Club and in Middlebury College he belonged to the choir. There he was a member of Chi Psi fraternity.

His companions respected his excellence in both studies and sports. They loved him for the qualities of his personality, a truthfulness that would not compromise, a keen sense of humor, his masculinity tempered with gentleness, his recognition of worth in others, and a modesty that never was affected by praise. I always knew it was a privilege to be Bill's mother.

Bill enlisted in the Navy Air Corps in the spring of 1942, and was called to service in August of that year. He trained at Squantum, Plymouth and Pensacola. He was commissioned a second lieutenant at Pensacola, March 1, 1943, and was the first in his class to be assigned to U. S. Marine Air Corps.

He came home then on furlough with orders to report to Cherry Point, N. C., for operational training on March 30th. One lovely month we enjoyed his company, then kissed him goodbye, and never saw him again.

On October 8, 1943, came the telegram with the news that he had crashed at Hilton-head Point in the vicinity of Parris Island at 3:30 on October 6th.

His body arrived home in a sealed casket on the tenth of October, escorted by Lt. H. Vern Hart, Bill's roommate. He and Bill had both received orders to report for commissioning as first lieutenants. Lt. Hart was later given the rank of captain. He told this story.

A squadron of four Corsair fighters, led by Major Day left Parris Island on a target practice at three o'clock. They had been out only a few minutes when orders were radioed that they should return. As the squadron turned about, a curious fog formation blotted the planes from each other's view. The first three arrived safely at Parris Island. No alarm was felt at Bill's absence until two hours had elapsed. Major Day, who later lost his earth life in the Pacific

9

area, wrote me that every man wanted to look for "Eric," as they called him. He had to order men to stay on the ground. The searching planes went up, fifty at a time, but it wasn't until two o'clock on the seventh that his own roommate, Lt. Hart, found him.

A coast-guard ship had radioed in that while watching a curious fog formation, a plane had been seen through a rift, spinning. That gave a clue.

By some miracle the plane did not crack-up completely. Bill had righted it, and had he been flying 500 feet higher, he could have made a safe landing. He was flying low, under orders. Neither did the plane burn. There was this highly inflammable octane gas, dripping on the hot motor, forming a pool for about thirty feet around the Corsair.

Bill was so well known on Staten Island that many people were shocked into the realization that there was a war. Letters and floral tributes poured in. Flags were at half-mast along the route from his home to Immanuel Church, Westerleigh, which was crowded for the service. Three members of the Marines formed a guard of honor. As he was borne out of the church, one of them blew taps. Then the cortege proceeded to the crematory at Linden.

Two days later, a navy plane, carrying his ashes circled his home and flew out to sea. At Miller field a squadron of planes rose to form an escort. His brother Dick, a sergeant ski-trooper, on leave from Camp Hale, Colorado, returned Bill's ashes to the elements.

Many, many mothers know only too well the period of grief at the separation. If Bill had been taken in battle, I could have understood it, but why had this happened, just as he had completed his training? His squadron, V.M.F. 312, was ready, waiting the order to go. I prayed through the nights for understanding, and my prayers were answered.

The following March, while visiting my daughter in Washington, I contacted a medium of great power. She called Bill, and wrote rapidly a list of thirty-seven names that he gave her to prove his survival of identity, and power of communication. Some were intimate family names, some were names of friends of his that I knew. Others were new to me. Upon returning home I found those names written on the backs of two group photographs, one of his Chi Psi fraternity, and one of his squadron at Parris Island. Had I known of the experiences that were to come to me, I would certainly have preserved that paper. He told me not to grieve so, for he had passed over without pain, was alive and well, and could come to me every night at 7:30 p.m. I was comforted at last, for I felt that I had visited with him. He no doubt tried to tell her other things which she didn't get, for very few mediums are absolutely perfect receiving stations.

My amazing experience came about a month later. Again, had I known what was to come, I would have written down the date. I am not naturally a statistician. I had just put my head upon the pillow one night and closed my eyes, when a bright curtain of light appeared, and in it grew a shining picture. A television picture is all I can compare it with. There sat Bill writing at a desk with his back to me. He was clothed in a white robe. Billowing white clouds encircled him. Surprise made me open my eyes. Then I could not recapture the picture. I wondered and wondered. Had I seen Bill in miniature? It wasn't a dream, because I am always a part of my dreams. This was objective and anyway I wasn't asleep.

A few nights later the experience was repeated. This time Bill stood in uniform before a blackboard, writing. I could not see what he wrote. Then he walked across the room, took his coat from a chair, opened a door, walked out, and the picture instantly vanished.

Another night there was a picture of a hand flipping a huge pile of papers.

There was some definite meaning to all this, and I knew that only a spiritual medium could explain it. So I visited Mrs.

Simon, a medium on Staten Island. She said it was very plain that my boy wanted to communicate with me through automatic writing.

I went home, sat at my desk, and held a pencil. An electric shock went through my arm and the pencil wrote so faintly and shakily, "My dear mother, my dear mother, I am so happy that you have made it possible for me to communicate with you in this way. I could be happy, but I cannot stand your tears." That stopped them.

The next time I wrote, he said he was happy because I was smiling. Then he tried to give me an evidential message. "Tell A. that I am with him and Manny in spirit." I had received a letter from A. expressing his sorrow at Bill's passing. That started a lovely correspondence. "Manny" was new to me. I wrote to A. who was a lieutenant in the air force in Italy, told him about my writing, and asked if Bill had such a friend. When his answer came, it was a disappointment. A. couldn't recall anyone by that name.

I told Bill about it and he wrote, "You will hear next week. A. will remember. All will come *clear*." Sure enough a letter came from A. the next week, dated Aug. 14, 1944. He wrote, "At first your 'Manny' had me wondering. Now it is all *clear*. Sure, there is a Manny, tho we rarely called him that, it was usually Mike. You see, Mike Mann and Bill and I always used to go around together. We generally had a foursome with Jack Bates. Mike was in my class at school, and is a Chi Psi, of course. He lives in Albany, N. Y., and is now in India serving with the U. S. Army Cavalry Corps. His real name is Joseph Henry Mann, Jr." So there I had evidence that although I wasn't always a good receiving station, it was Bill doing his best to give me evidential messages.

Since the purpose of this book is to "Show the world that the spirit survives and can communicate" (Bill's words) I must tell about the things Mrs. Ella Tellier told me and also about Rev. Glenn Argoe.*

_____
* Bill spoke through Miss Argoe and from the things he said, left no doubt in my mind that it was he.

I had decided to contact a medium to verify my communications. I was impressed with the messages, given by Mrs. Tellier, one Sunday afternoon at a meeting of The Spiritual and Ethical Society, held at the Hotel Astor. I telephoned her, and she gave me an appointment for a sitting. It began at 7:00 p.m. I told her nothing about Bill. Her guides brought messages from my mother, father and grandmother. I was waiting tensely, watching the big clock over her head. At exactly 7:30 she said, "Here comes a William who calls you 'Mother'." Bill told me later that he had timed his visit to make it more evidential. He told her many evidential things. One of them was about how pleased he was that I had made a scrapbook containing photographs of him, clippings in the local and high school papers referring to his activities, his graduation programs, report cards, poems he had written as a child, etc.

I made three visits to Mrs. Tellier. The last one made a deep impression on me. It happened that the night preceding this visit, which had been arranged for about two weeks in advance, an old friend of ours committed suicide by shooting himself through the roof of the mouth. Mrs. Tellier described this man perfectly, gave his first name, and then said in astonishment, "Why this is a confused spirit. He doesn't know what this is all about. He points to his mouth and doesn't speak. He followed the path of light opened up when my guides called your friends. One of them is going to take him to his wife and parents." Spiritualists say that no one comes to meet a suicide. Bill told me later that it was a lucky thing for this man that I went to Mrs. Tellier on that day.

No more pictures came until the night before Memorial Day. That was beautiful beyond description. It was shining silver. Huge wings in a relief design formed the background. That would symbolize aviation. In the center a boy was embracing a mother. In the lower foreground, four dear little angel heads with curly hair bobbed

17

and smiled at me. I was enchanted with it and will always keep it in my memory.

One night he showed me a beautiful large living room. I saw a flowered rug, rose curtains before a long window and some easy chairs. I wondered what it was. Bill told me at my next writing that he was showing me his living room. He said he couldn't make it as clear as he wished. "There should have been a big table in the center, a chest of drawers in the window, and a picture of angels hanging by the window."

Recently, he gave me a picture of a soldier boy sitting alone in a room. He told me it was a picture of a Chi Psi boy who came over not so long ago. He is trying to give me his name, so that I can tell his folks. I haven't yet the power to get names straight. I seem to put up a mental wall when a name comes. I write it and the pencil says, "No." I'm praying for that power.

The last picture I had showed a little black dog. The next day my son arrived with his wife and boys and a new little black dog. When I had time to write, Bill told me he had heard Dick planning to come. "So I thought it would be fun to make a picture of the little dog, and it wasn't bad, do you think? That was how I was telling you that Dick was coming."

The writing came more fluently. Bill said he had progressed so that he could see vast distances and many people at once. He was enjoying this greater freedom so much.

Later . . .

"You will have a delightful surprise in the beginning of the year, 1946. The masters are preparing a book which I am allowed to give to you. It is to show that the spirit survives and can communicate. It will tell the world the thought of God. It will be written in simple language that all can understand. It will be short so that the price will be small. It is meant to reach people all over the world. As soon as it is ready, I will dictate it to you, and when I tell you, you are to give it to the world. Get plenty of paper, and have the pencils sharpened to a fine point. Take time to sit to God each day, and think of His goodness. Then pray for power. I cannot think that you will not make the effort."

On January 10, 1946, came the command, "Sit right, Mom. Keep your arm off the table, so I won't have to push so hard. Now is the time. The title is *A Story of a Boy Who Came Home*."

The story, as it appeared on the paper, amazed me as much as it will surprise any of its readers. Sometimes I couldn't keep up with it mentally, the writing went so fast. Two of the chapters, each had a break of some days before I found opportunity to continue. I didn't read the previous notes before sitting. When I put them together, there was perfect continuity.

Bill stressed the fact that the book is the thought of the masters. "It is being reviewed by the spirit world. Let no one change it, not a word. It is the truth as it stands. You were very receptive when the book was being given."

Later . . .

"I think the people will take the book

to heart. Then the time will be ripe for more revelations which the teachers will let me give. They will be given when people can take them. The way to work for God is to work for the soul's redemption. Think only of the great privilege it is to serve in this way. It is the most blessed way to serve, to help spread the truth."

Later . . .

"The blue heaven is the place where we hold forth. It is in the heaven that these things take place. It is the place where nothing is hid. It sounds awful to say, 'Souls of the departed,' when it isn't true. They never went far. We like to have you know that we live with you, but so the world cannot see us. It isn't right that they should, for then they couldn't tend to their earth affairs. It would be too blundering to think that people could live in two worlds at once. It would mix things up, so in the wisdom of God, the worlds cannot be together in sight, and yet they can be together in every other way. We tell you things to do so that the results will make you happy, and we tell you what to think, so the life will be clear to the mind.

Later . . .

"I am the mind of happiness to see the men think of the truth in this book, and to think that the Lord gave me the power to bring it to the world. It is such a privilege to serve the Lord. It is the acme of joy to see the men think of the book to their comfort. I can tell you it is the love to the world that makes possible the works of love. It is the time to come close to the truth, to the thought of minding the mysteries of creation. I am the happy one to tell the world to be ready for the kingdom of God. I am in the light to this work. I am the mind of hope to the world. There is nothing to mental thought but the love of God. It is the thought of this love that brings health to the world. I can tell the world to be well, but the world must believe the love of God that places health in their bodies to be the thought that it must stay there."

Later . . .

"This book is the love of God to the thought of helping His children."

December 25, 1946 . . .

"Now is the time to put forth the book, helping those who are in doubt. Let the book speak for itself. Love is the theme of it, love is the success of it. The love is the proof and the love is the power."

Chapter One

COMING HOME

I saw a bright light in the sky on the sixth of October, 1943. I started to turn off the motor. Then the light seemed brighter, so I said to myself, "That is queer, it must be getting a bit stormy."

So the time passed, and I thought, "This is not the right direction. I should be going south, and this is north." Then I saw a ship in the ocean. I said, "I should not be near the ocean." So I turned around and started for the south. Then the currents took me to the east. I said, "This is not the way." But I couldn't stop going that way.

Then the scene changed, and the whole sky was full of people who called to me, "You are coming home, so keep coming."

I thought, "This is queer. Who are these people? They don't know where I should go. What are they doing here anyway?" I started to turn, but someone held me on the course. I said, "Please let me go."

The people called louder, "You come home!"

"I can't come home, for I don't live near here."

They said, "Yes, this is your home."

I almost cried with worry, for I wanted to reach my squadron. I tried to turn back, and couldn't.

Then a woman came close to me, and said, "I am your grandmother.* You never knew me, but I have watched over you for a long time." She said, "You are Bill Ericson," and I said, "You are my mother's mother."

"Yes, but you never saw me before. I

_____
* Charlotte Hjelm Forssell

think it is so good that I can come to meet you, for otherwise you would be lost."

I said, "I think I am lost now."

She said, "No, you soon will be home."

Then a voice said, "You tell me how you could be lost when I can take you home."

It was Pop.* I knew him at once. I said, "But you are dead." Mom, he said, "You are wrong there, my boy. I never was so alive in the whole span of my existence. I see you think we tell lies when we tell about the future life. You have just passed the line, my boy."

Then I stood there trying to think. "Did I think this all up, or has it happened?"

"I thought of you, Mom, and what you said to me, that a thousand might fall, but no harm would come to me! So I sat down and cried because I couldn't tell you about what had happened to me. I saw the earth so far away. I couldn't see the people, but I could hear the sound of weeping.

I said, "I must get to my mother," but

* Bill's grandfather Gustav Forssell

26

the spirits around me said, "Not yet. You are tired. You need rest, so wait, and we will take you soon."

So I went to the place where new spirits are led, and there I saw my old friends from Parris Island. There was my old pal holding me in his arms, and saying, "Gee, my mamma thinks I am dead, and it is the very thing I am not."

I said, "My mother thinks I am alive, and I shall try to let her know how right she is."

So I came at last to this house. I couldn't make you see me, but I called to your mind, and made you get the idea that I could write through your hand. It wasn't at all easy at first, for you couldn't get my meaning many times. You never got discouraged. You just tried again, and now you really do get my thoughts, but not names. That surely will come too. Now I will stop. I will come with the next chapter when you are ready. Bill."

Chapter Two

COMMUNICATION AND
THE LAWS

I came to this house and saw you weeping, not because I was dead, but because you no longer could see me or touch me. So I went to the first teacher in my plane and asked how I could communicate with you.

He said it was all a matter of electricity. You see it takes power to make power, so he helped me to tell you that I wanted to write.

He made those pictures of me which amazed you so. Then he thought of the way to make you understand them. He gave you the idea of asking Mrs. Simon. So that worked out fine.

Mom, it gave me the thrill of my life when you first sat down to write. You didn't get it all clear, but you got the gist of the message, which was that I was so happy that you had made it possible for me to communicate with you, and that it was the greatest joy to see you smile again. It came off so well.

Other things came clear like the message that A. would write to you that he remembered who was meant by "Manny." I really gave you "Mike" but you didn't get it, so it didn't register with A. at first. A. sure was a good sport to help you like that. He is indeed my good pal, for someone else might have just thought you daffy, and ignored your request. So it all came out as we planned it here. You amused us so many times with the words you wrote. We couldn't figure where they came from. But the mistakes were ours as much as yours.

It isn't easy to tell you how this works,

but I must try. It is as though a wire is charged with electricity and then placed in my cap, and connected with your mind. I see you don't understand "cap." It is the mind name up here. I see that amuses you. Well, it is funny too, for it isn't outside our heads by any means. I can tell you we do not use it to think with. We use the heart. Isn't that strange?

The heart is the thought center of the spirit body. That is why the heart is referred to so often in books, really as the mind. I can tell you that the thoughts of the heart are the most lasting too. I see yours, and they really are the best you have. I see your mind too, and it is good, but your heart is better. I see you really wanting to do some good thing; then your head tells the heart it is silly. So you obey the head, which in your case, is the second best.

I tell you this, so that you will understand when I say, "Obey your heart."

I tell the boys here that they would make the earth the finest thing in creation, if they would tell their folks about this life, and how to prepare for it. We could hasten the millenium which has to come, because it's God's law.

We learn the laws soon after we get here. A teacher instructs us. The first one is to love; the most difficult, I think, because we all seem so selfish. The second one is to help, and that is easier. It doesn't matter who it is, you can help without loving them. The third one is to think the right thought, which is also very hard, for it is so simple to just condemn what we think unpleasant.

I sat near the teacher, and watched his face. He was really beautiful to watch. His eyes shone with love. It seemed to lighten all around him. He stood up and raised his arms. Then he said, "The peace of God is now in you, so be not afraid. You never more will see the sights of cruelty you saw on earth. The love of God is in you. You never more will wish to shoot or kill. You are now the blessed in God, and the servants of his people; so tell the world to love, to help, to think right, and earth will soon be the paradise God made it.

"Now go back to the earth and do what you can. You do the deeds that come your way, and then come here to rest, and enjoy the beauties of this heaven."

So down we came into the thick of the fighting, and told the boys to come along with us for a while, when they were killed, so to speak. Some were thrilled, but some called us names, and told us to go to hell, as we tried to persuade them to leave the battle. They kept right on fighting until we just overpowered them, and brought them up. Then we talked to them until the light broke, and it was lovely to see the joy in their faces when they found themselves living after all that destruction.

I tell you, Mom, it was the finest feeling in my life, when I could convince some boy that he had come home, instead of dying. It surely was a blessed task the teacher gave us.

I used to wonder what you would say if you knew what your boy was thinking, and doing.

32

Chapter Three

THE TELL-TALE AURA

In the tell-tale aura of all people are the sins they have committed. If they atone for the sins before leaving the earth, the stains are removed. None should come to heaven in fear. It is true that there will be the time of the mind of sorrow for some who come here, thinking the thoughts of selfishness, but when they find the mind of repentance, the souls purge themselves of their sins. It is not in the dark, but in the light of God's love.

The punishment is the shame that people feel when others see their sins. It is the thought of others knowing one's inmost failings that is so terrible to bear. It is hard to see the disappointment manifested by those who come to meet one they think so good, and then see the evidence that he is just a sinner. It will not happen to anyone who is ready to believe that the Lord will forgive the sins of those who repent, and try to lead a life of service.

It isn't so much what is done in the way of atonement, as how it is done. Do good, give to those who need, secretly. Don't go thinking how good you are. The things that count so much on earth don't mean a thing here. It is what you stand for that makes you important or not. So think good thoughts, do good deeds, and believe that Jesus is the very Son of God, and you will come to the joys that you couldn't ever imagine. It is something that passes the comprehension of the mortal mind.

You will then meet the higher spirits who live nearest to God. It is a much better plane in every way, for then you can see so far, and do so many things that you couldn't do on the other planes. The truth is that the tell-tale aura must be washed before you can enter the presence of the Lord. It is so very important to know this. The world needs this message. There are many who are complacent, thinking so many things really do not matter so much. I tell you they do. People should beware of idle talk. No one should judge another. One should not harbor the tiniest bit of malice. Think only of the wonderful things of God's creation.

I saw the whole world as in a nutshell. It is a marvelous creation. The stars which seem colorless are bright and colorful. There are green, red, orange, blue; in fact all the colors of the rainbow. I tell you it is something one can never describe, but it just is, that's all. The plan of the universe is the plan of God who is in it all the time. I cannot see God, but His presence is felt by all of us. His complete love fills everything. The brightness of it is indescribable, so you wonder how you stand the light. I cannot make you even guess at the quality of this light, but it is so intense that at first

35

you don't see anything but many colors. It fills me with the most complete ecstacy. It couldn't be imagined.

There is a sense of complete security, of peace, of joy beyond the mind of man to comprehend. I see the happiness reflected in the faces of those about me. It should make the life on earth more meaningful to know that this awaits those who keep the laws of God. There is the fullest comple-tion, so that you never regret the coming here, since this has all that earth can offer, and then so much more.

It is wrong to wish back into the mortal body, a soul come home. This is the best way for me to be. It is the first idea of God. The body is the last thing to be thought of. It is the temple, but it isn't the real person that the Lord has made to be eternal. It is the temporary home. That's the truth. So you shouldn't wish me back in it. You should come to me. Try to reach the heights. Think of your coming up, not my going down.

All churches are true that teach the

people to try to rise to God, to repent of their sins. All churches are true that teach the beautiful truth that Jesus is the true Son of God. It will be wonderful when there is unity in the church of God.

I see the world being more ready to accept the truth, for the times will make it necessary for people to come closer to God. The world will always have new testimony to help the truth to spread.

I hope the world will take this book to heart. Then the time will be ripe for more revelations which the teachers will let me give, as they see that people can take them.

Chapter Four

THE RIGHT PRAYER

In the land of spirits, many seek to find peace and cannot because they persist in thinking they are on the earth, and haven't the plenty of earth. They wish to do the same things they did on earth, and they try to tell us that there is no such place as heaven anywhere. We tell them about the higher planes, but they do not believe us, and will not try to reach them; so then there is nothing to do but let them stay until they decide at last to try to progress. Such spirits are called earthbound.

They are not necessarily evil, but they do not do any good. They cannot harm anyone either. The reason they do the things they do, is that they never, while on earth, believed in any hereafter or in God. So it isn't right for us to condemn them and ignore them. Some will not pray either, so no one comes to them to help them.*

It is wonderful what prayer will do. In fact the very thought of prayer uplifts us all. So keep praying for us, all of us; just to make us feel that you come to us in that mysterious bond that no one really understands.

If you find time to pray, you will find time for the many things you wish you had time for now.

I see the best things in life going to the prayerful, when they pray with faith; not crying in misery, but in the sure knowledge that help will come. Come close to true prayer. Smile when you pray.

Now this is the right way. Just say the Lord's prayer and nothing else. Not another thing should you ask for. It takes in everything the heart should desire. The

* At first this seemed to me to be a contradiction, but now I understand. They can be told, but not helped till they pray —E ε

plentiful gifts of life will come when you say, "Give us this day our daily bread." It isn't asking just for food. It's the genuine desire to come closer to the life of Christ, the Son of God. It means the whole thinking should be about the spiritual things, not the material; for they come if the others are achieved. It isn't the thought of asking God just for the things the physical body needs, for He supplies them without your asking.

It is the eternal things you must acquire for yourself, like love, charity, proper thinking, and true living to the glory of God. It isn't the bread of the physical body, but the bread of the spirit that you should ask for, that you must work for, and then if you really mean to try to live for it, you surely will receive the things you want most in the earth life too.

It seems to me so very marvelous that it should be the first message that Jesus really gave. He said, "I am the bread of life. Come unto me and be filled." Isn't that the essence of it all? I see the whole meaning

40

of life charged with new beauty, new power, new intelligence, and trust in God. So do not pray for money or treasure of earthly sort, but for the treasures of the spirit. It will bring you all that you could desire.

It isn't the first time this has been said, but the truth can stand repeating again and again. It is eternal! It is the blest message of Jesus. It is the very millenium of the soul. It is the faith in the Lord.

I can think of nothing more important to the people of earth. It is my mission to help spread the truth. That is the reason the Lord called me home. So help me to be a message-bearer and truth-bringer of this time. Go now to your many tasks in the knowledge that you must be a worker for God's truth. The world must again hear the message, "I am the bread of life. Come unto me and be filled."

Chapter Five

PARTNERS WITH GOD

I came to the third plane. This is not a permanent home. It is a place of rest for those who intend to go on. I stayed a short time. Then I started to progress.

I came to a place of beauty with springs and trees whose loveliness can't be described. Here too I stayed a short time. I saw the mansions of people who were remaining here because it seemed to them the very best.

The scene then changed for me, a scene so gorgeous, there is nothing with which I can compare it. Everything glitters and gives out such light that the underworld is made invisible. It thrilled me to go about, looking at the mansions. Many masters live in them. They stay to teach the people who wish to learn about the mansions of the higher spheres. I built myself a mansion and lived in it so very comfortably. There wasn't much to do at first, so I came to the masters and absorbed their teachings. If you think you can go higher, you are allowed to study.

I could then take the mansion with me to the next plane. The beauty of life here is far above that of the lower plane. It is the most pleasant place, for all the people tell the others the pleasantest thoughts. They see so much good in everyone else. We have meetings where we sing and dance. Often we come together to smile, nothing else. The light of God shines on us. It shines on the earth too, brighter than the world dreams of. There is a wonder that sings in the heart as I gaze upon it, no matter how often I see it. So many close their eyes to this brightness. It is the time to come to the realization of the blessings that so many tell themselves don't exist. The blessings that the Lord gives can be taken by all, not just a few. The blessed of the Lord will have the most of the world's goods as well as the treasures of heaven. First acquire the things of heaven. Then the others will be given.

Mom, I have seen Jesus. The most wonderful thing about Him is His simplicity. He is the most pleasant, approachable Spirit here. He is the kindest, the gentlest that one could imagine. He goes the whole length of creation and is the guiding Spirit of it all. I tell you that the way people have distorted His message is the trouble today. He says that the backbone of the brotherhood of man is to try to serve, to put no person below you, to try to uplift all others, to try to see good in everyone, and to tell the people about the love of God that shines right on us all. It is so true that what we do for people is done for God, for He is right in us. It is wonderful to feel that as we do here. The more we try to help, the easier it becomes. God is near you when the thing is good, but not when it isn't. That is the law of God, for evil is not near Him in any way. To be good is to be near God. This is really the whole thought of this book. Atone for your sins, win redemption and enter into undreamed of joy.

There is no other one who sees God but Jesus, so you will never see Him, but in His presence you live and move and have your being. It is an awe-inspiring thought, the fact of being part of the Infinite Intelligence. The truth is so terribly astounding that you can do the things that Jesus does, if you don't think the truth is impossible. Just think it is, and then the power will come to you. The thought to have is that God is the power, not you or anyone else. Be thankful when you have power to do good, but don't take credit to yourself.

We are partners with God, for He has endowed us with powers so that we can work miracles like Jesus. The world should come to an understanding of these powers. They come when the soul makes peace with God, when the heart is free from all ill-will toward anyone. Then if the soul turns to God and says, "Thy will be done on earth as it is in heaven," the healing power courses through the mind and body, and the cure is accomplished. Pray that way, and you will be able to help others even if they don't believe it. This is the way to come close to the power of God. It is so very inspiring that nothing will seem more comfortable than to sit and commune with Him. Then light will be around you, and others will feel the benefit of it without being aware. Just by being good, you shed blessings upon others.

Chapter Six

RIGHT THINKING

I cannot think why so many people believe that the thought of the mind is the best; for the thought of the heart is the true one. It is the heart that thinks, but scientists say it is the brain. The thought that comes from the heart is the true one, complete with the mind of God. It tells us when we do wrong, and when we please God. The thought of the living God comes into it, and stays there.

The mind is the thought of the mortal man. It is influenced by the thought of so many other peoples' minds, but the thought of the heart is the thought of the self that

47

we are. It is the thought of the self that God put into each one of us. I see it is a strange idea to you too, but think upon it, and understanding will come.

The heart cannot be changed except by the mind. The mind influences it to the extent that we very often think it is our hearts telling us to tell the truth, when it is the mind telling us to tell a falsehood. It is the thought of the heart that thinks of the good to do, but the mind so often changes the thought to the idea of the wrong, that the very soul is influenced by it. That is the way the many wickednesses come to be in existence.

It is the thought to be made clear that the mortal mind is the cause of the sickness, the poverty, and the wickedness on earth.

It is not a new thought, for the Christian Scientists have that truth. There are so many truths that the many sects are telling, but it seems that most of them believe in the idea that trouble is sent by God to chasten them. That is so false, it is the thought of the mind.

48

But the heart tells that God is love, and the love of God will therefore bring you out of all trouble. So spread this message, and tell the world that the way to be the perfect image of God is to think that the troubles come from the mind of man, and can be cured by the heart of God.

If they make their peace with that thought of God's mind being the only real mind, and man's mind being the thought of the thinking God, then they will feel the véry spirit of God flowing through their thoughts, and trouble will disappear.

The spirit life, the life of the thought of God is the real life. It tells the thought of God, it tells the way to progress to the highest. So think the thoughts of the Lord to bring peace. The thinking is the thing. It is so very important to think right. That is what brings the right help.

The earth is the place where the soul thinks of the life to come; the life that is the real life. It is true that so many other influences try to take the soul to themselves that it isn't easy. But the thought of helping, the thought of trying to uplift is the one that will in the end be the victor. The trying to help will bring the mastery over these other forces. It is the law of God that the truth will in the end prevail over evil.

Evil is the littlest thing in the world. It is the most insignificant, and the least to be feared. It will be most completely abolished when men come to think right. It is the very essence of right thinking to discredit the powers of evil. It is the flower of life that comes to the man who thinks only good thoughts. It is so necessary to feel the mind of God working through the body. Then the troubles of life will disappear.

It is the thought of God's mind being the only mind that brings peace to the body as well as the soul. Then the thought of evil simply cannot enter the heart. It is the idea to impress upon the world that there is only one mind. That is the truth. It is clear then that the mind that thinks the God thoughts might do the God works. This is the thought that brings the right between the Creator and His creation. This is the way to think. I am the child of God. God is in me. If it is so, then no harm can come to me. It is so simple as that.

The trouble is that people just won't make the attempt to reach God. It is He who is trying to reach them, but they go away from Him. It is sad to see the lives pleased to take the wrong way instead of the right. It is sad to see the people suffering when it is so unnecessary. It is sad to see those whom the Lord is helping the most, not listening to His voice. It is the saddest thing to see the little children who do not know the truth about God. It makes even the angels weep. It is the thought of God that the children should be taught. But the parents neglect the thought themselves, so how can they then teach their children? It is sad to hear people saying there is no God, when He is trying to tell them of His love. It is too bad the world isn't with Him. Then so much sorrow could be avoided.

It is so true that there need be no sickness if the world is conscious of the power of God. There need be no poverty if people think of God as their supply. There need be no evil if people see that God is all, and God is good. So the whole thing is the presence of God in the world. He is the essence of the world, and the power of it. The evil has no power. It is the least significant as the many spirits can tell you. The trouble is that so many people prefer to think the evil thought that the better one is submerged.

The thought of God removes evil, but the thought of evil cannot remove God. You ask, "Why can't God just put evil out of the world?" The truth is that there is no evil except in man's mortal mind. That is the truth. It isn't so bad when storms come, but the way people think of it is bad. The mind seems to see more evil than is caused by storms. The houses blown down should not be made the thought of trouble, for they can be built up better the next time. The people who seem to be destroyed do not die. They come to the home of God.

So there is no trouble that the Hand of God cannot make into a blessing. Mind is the trouble-maker, not God. Now there is the truth that the soul of man is the idea of God, so it is the God idea that should be kept uppermost in the mind. But people tell themselves that they are the men they make themselves, that God put them here to work out their own salvation. That isn't so. They are the God idea, that is the mind of God. So they must live in the mind of God to be the very mind of God. That is the whole truth if the world can only grasp it. It isn't so easy to say they must, but that is so.

The way to work miracles is to think, "I am the very mind of God. There is nothing I cannot bring to pass, for His being is one with mine. The blessing of God be on this work, so that the blessing of God come on this soul." Then the miracle is wrought. The love of God is with you now and always.

Bill.

Chapter Seven

ALL-POWER BLESSING

I see the people telling you that they see the truth in this book. It is the cause of the people. I can help by making these communications the thing of mind to the world.

I see the people thinking of the place of spirits in the wrong way. They should know the truth, so they can prepare themselves for this more lasting life. I call this place, Heaven, but it is The Land of Spirits, the land where spirits live like the people on earth. It is more real than the earth world, for the things of this land cannot be the thought of destruction like those on earth.

I see the minds of people being affected by the thoughts of the minds of a few instead of thinking for themselves. I must tell people to think for themselves, and be unafraid to tell their thoughts in the light of love and freedom. I can see the world making progress in that direction. I can see them being more helpful to each other and making more progress in the way of minding the thought of love. I see them telling the world that the thought of the love of God is the thing to keep most in mind. Then the love of the Son of God for He is the true Son who sees the father. I told that before, but it must be stressed. I see the change come when people think of the love of Jesus, for He rests in the power of God. I can see Him.

It is the love of God that lets us think the thoughts of love to people. It is the love of God that keeps people from the things of the mind of Ananias, for the truth is God's law, and those who break it will suffer. There is no escape from that.

I see the world being more clean in their thoughts too, for that is necessary to their advancement in the mind of truth. I see the world thinking more about the powers they have from God. They can be more mind of mental light and strength where now they stumble blindly on. I can see them being powerful minds to be the workers of miracles when their minds come to the mind of God. I can tell the world to be powerful. I can tell the world to be spiritual, but they never will be until they put off the mind of selfishness, and put on the mind of love. I see them thinking it isn't necessary to be unselfish, but they never can reach the mind of God, till it is themselves they think of last. I make that statement with mind of emphasis.

I see the time when a child will be the thought of mind of God, the thought of love and called mind of All-Mind. The child will come without pain. The child will come without the conference of the medical mind. The child will come without the thought of trouble, but with joy unspeakable. I can tell the world it will come to pass.

The love of God will keep people from the love of evil. I see the time when there will be no pleasure in evil. Then the lives will be happy. The lives will be sure in the love of God. I can see the time when the thought of the Mind of God will keep out the thought of sin. It is sin that shuts God out of our lives, but repentance brings Him back if we are sincere in the desire to be better. The soul of the sinner can be redeemed only by sincere repentance, but it will be the love of God that makes him repent.

The thought that keeps the world from sin is the thought of wishing to please God. Until people think of God in their lives the whole time, they cannot come to be minds of God. The thought is the love that makes people try to love the sinning one as well as the upright. The love that wishes to help, not to condemn. That will keep the world from the thought of evil. Those who think that way will be the powerful ones to work miracles. When they pray for that power, it will come.

I can see the world not thinking anything is impossible. The thought of the power of God can bring them the things they wish on earth, as well as the spiritual things. Those who had so much on earth that they never prayed to God will find their spiritual assets very meager. They will find their life here arduous till they learn to think of the things of God as the first to be minded. I can tell the world that Jesus meant what he said in the sermon on the mount, for the poor are the blessed in this life. The thought of the things of earth will be the hindrance here till their insignificance becomes the thought of their minds. The time is here when the mind of man needs this message more than ever.

The world must be the thought of love. I see men thinking that the powers of evil will wreck this place of abode, but it will never come to pass that evil will triumph over God, for He is the Mind of the world. He is the Power, so where is the mind that can triumph over the Only Mind? He is the Power that will make the world the paradise it is to be.

Think of the idea of God being All. That will help to solve the problems. The thought of the allness of His love is the thought that will make the desires be granted. I see the problems solved when people think this way. I see the problems not coming to the mind that already has this thought. There is the thought that the love of God is with us the entire time of existence, so the flower of life is to the one who is conscious of this fact. It keeps the trouble thoughts in the background. Then they disappear.

It is the anthology of love that is found in the psalms of David. They should be often read. They bring the thoughts of God's love so vividly to the mind. He was the true lover of God in his time. There is the proof that in every age some soul is the thought of love to God to be the inspiration to the world.

It is time to be continuously thinking of the power of God, for His power is in us to the thought there is nothing impossible if we believe it to be possible. The teeth need not be extracted, but can be kept whole and clean in the thought of God's power. It is true of the eyes too. People think the teeth and eyes must be the thought of the professions, so they mind the thought of their decay, instead of minding the thought of their health. To be the mind of All-power is to think nothing need be the thought of the mind of destruction.

I can tell the world to think spiritually but their thoughts go to the material. Then when trouble comes, they do not consider the love of God, so they do not feel it the way a soul does that has thought of the amazing love of God, the powerful Father. God cannot be All-power and then let his children suffer. I can tell you it is cause for rejoicing among us when the soul thinks the thought of love to the world. I tell you it will be the blessing of God on the one who tells the world to love. Truth and affliction cannot live together.

Life about us here is glorious. It is full of All-power and is the mind of love to the minds of all here. We work, we communicate, we deliver messages to tell the world —all that they are able to understand. All-mind gives us the thoughts to work out to make the world the place of beauty that it is. We sing in chorus, we have time to read and time to amuse ourselves in any manner we choose, and time to rest when the amount of work allotted to us is completed. I am asking for the mind of missionary work because the need is so great. It is the most important to Mind of All-Power that All Power should come to His creation. I can see All Power coming to the people who are All-Mind of God. I can tell the world there is nothing impossible to men who live in the Mind of God.

The Mind of God is not to be the mind of selfish power, but it is the unselfish love to the world. No one will ever acquire power with God who is the mind of ego and cannot subserviate his own mind to that of God. I see the time when this is the common teaching to children. Then they never start to put ideas of All-Mind away and substitute the mind of Ananias. They can think only good thoughts because the idea of evil is never brought before them. It is this Mind that should be cultivated to the love of the world, and then all peace will come to the clearing mind of this world. All, all is God. All is all in God. All must be the peace of God. All is the love of God.

The power is the thought of mind that realizes the infinite power of God. There is nothing that it cannot make to pass, so this understanding then will enter the consciousness to the degree that the mind is full of confidence in God's power, not just hope, but sure knowledge that the power is there. I can tell the world there is nothing that the good soul desires that it will not receive, because good is one with God.

Do the thinking this way—I wish the Lord to be the thought of bringing this to pass. I know the Lord will bring it to pass. I thank Thee, Lord, for having heard me.

It is the strongest prayer that is made in confidence. The thought of failure will please the mind of Ananias but not the Mind of God. I can tell the world to think this way and All-Power will be with them. I conclude by saying, "The power of God be with you to be the truth-bringer to the World."

Bill.

CPSIA information can be obtained
at www.ICGtesting.com
Printed in the USA
BVOW03*0618310817

493568BV00004B/8/P